Praise for
Empowered by Praise
by Michael Youssef

"Michael Youssef has provided yet another great guide to worshiping our Lord with the tools for understanding and incorporating the empowering dynamics of praise in your daily walk with Christ."

—CHARLES W. COLSON, chairman,
Prison Fellowship Ministries

"Praise is the means by which God's rule and presence may be invited into the midst of any situation or circumstance. Michael Youssef capably leads us in the adventure of praise that is the means to life-delivering power and Spirit-enhancing grace."

—JACK W. HAYFORD, Litt.D., pastor
of the Church on the Way

"The psalmist wrote, 'I will bless the Lord at all times; His praise shall continually be in my mouth.' It sounds wonderful, high, lofty, but is it possible? How is praise lived out? What practical difference will it make in my life? Michael's book, *Empowered by Praise,* could give you a whole new lease on your day-by-day walk with your God and Savior."

—KAY ARTHUR, co-CEO,
Precept Ministries International

"Thank you, Michael! I am so grateful for a book that not only gives a strong theological basis for why we praise and worship God but also gives practical ways that can be applied to life."

—DON MOEN, executive vice president/
creative director of Integrity Music

"Michael Youssef's *Empowered by Praise* speaks to the heart in a fresh, exciting, and practical way. A must-read book for every believer, from the heart of a praising pastor."

—CLIFF BARROWS, music and program
director, Billy Graham Evangelistic Team

I PRAISE

You,

O GOD

Experiencing His Power
in Your Private Worship

MICHAEL YOUSSEF

WATERBROOK
PRESS

I PRAISE YOU, O GOD
PUBLISHED BY WATERBROOK PRESS
2375 Telstar Drive, Suite 160
Colorado Springs, Colorado 80920
A division of Random House, Inc.

ISBN 1-57856-557-X

Library of Congress Cataloging-in-Publication Data
    Youssef, Michael.
        I praise you, o God : experiencing His power in your private worship /
    by Michael Youssef.— 1st ed.
            p. cm.
        ISBN 1-57856-557-X
    1. Praise of God. 2. Christian life. I. Title.
        BV4817 .Y68 2002
        248.3—dc21

                                                        2002006907

Printed in the United States of America
2002—First Edition

10 9 8 7 6 5 4 3 2 1

CONTENTS

PRAISE HIM WITH PASSION

Praise the Lord!

If King David were with us today, I have no doubt he would sound this clarion call to every believer using those very words: *Praise the Lord!* He would encourage us to clap our hands, to make a joyful noise to almighty God with musical instruments, and to shout praises to the Most High! That's right, *shout!* And David wouldn't quietly stand before us, meekly offering this as a suggestion for us to consider. No, he would be animated; he would *implore* us to join him and all the saints of God in praising our Lord.

To our Western way of thinking, this might seem a bit

overbearing. But let me help you see things from David's perspective. I am by birth and by upbringing a Middle Easterner, so I understand this man's passion. In the Middle East, you don't greet a friend with a casual hello. Even if you have just seen that friend the day before, you greet him warmly when you see him again. Often, you will embrace him. Encountering a friend is a cause for gladness.

How much more, then, would a Middle Easterner such as David express his feelings when encountering the Lord Most High, the God who loves us far more than any friend ever could? You can imagine that the praise, the expressions of joy and gladness, the words of honor, all these would far exceed the warm greetings exchanged by good friends. So you can understand why, if David were here today, he would insist that we put our hearts into our praise of God.

If David walked into your worship service this Sunday, he wouldn't rest until everyone was on their feet, singing, playing instruments, dancing. Or, depending on the occasion, David might compel us to lie facedown on the ground, humbly confessing to God His greatness, His faithfulness, His glory. David would insist that we grant God the glory and honor and adoration that only He deserves and that we do it in humility and with *passion.*

So if David were here…would you gladly heed his call to praise God with your entire being—all that you are, all that you have, and all that you will ever be—every day of your life?

WHAT PRAISE CREATES

As a new believer, C. S. Lewis had great trouble with the Bible's commands to praise God. He wrote,

> We all despise the man who demands continued assurance of his own virtue, intelligence, and delightfulness. And these words of the Scripture sounded hideous, like God was saying, "What I want most is to be told that I am good and I am great." It also seemed as if the psalm writers were bargaining with God. "God, do you like praise? Well, do this or do that and I will give you some praise."[1]

As Lewis grew in his faith, however, he learned the importance of a daily surrender to the lordship of Jesus Christ. That's when he came to a new understanding of the importance of praise, reflecting these thoughts in his writing: "Only in the act of worship and praise can a person learn to believe in the goodness and the greatness of God. God wants us to praise him, not because he needs or craves, in any sense, our flattery. But because he knows that praise creates joy and thankfulness."[2]

I regularly encounter Christians who regard praise as something we do for God. They believe that when we praise God, we somehow bring Him benefit. In truth, we praise God because

---

1. C. S. Lewis, *Reflections on the Psalms* (San Diego: Harvest Book/Harcourt, 1986), 90.

2. Adapted from Lewis, *Reflections on the Psalms*, 93-5.

in doing so, we put ourselves into a position to receive benefit and blessing from Him. Praise results in great changes in us, in those we love, and in the world around us. Praise produces spiritual growth and development. Praise is the great engine that drives the church forward, resulting in greater faith as we pray, a more powerful witness, and amazing victories in the spiritual realm.

But praise is not a program by which we manipulate God to answer our prayer requests. No! Praise flows naturally from our relationship of love and devotion to the Lord.

Praise is more than an obligation, more than a simple spiritual exercise. Praise is the path that brings us near to God and His love, His power, and His grace. It brings us closer to the throne of God, to a more intimate relationship with our Creator, Savior, and Lord, and to a more fulfilling life on this earth.

Every person I know, in the depths of his or her heart, seeks a life of fulfillment and joy. We are driven to know our reason for being. We want our lives to make a difference, to bring out something of lasting value. As the saying goes, we don't want much— we want everything, at least everything that matters.

God is that everything. To find a life of meaning, we need to concentrate on praising Him. Not only does praise put us in closer communion with God, it also reveals things to us about ourselves. Praise opens our eyes to spiritual reality, to the love and power of God, and to our desperate need for Him.

Praise is an adventure—an empowering adventure. In praising God, we have a chance to really know who we are, and we begin to experience the great mystery and power of God's work on this earth.

This is the greatest exhilaration a person can know.

YOUR UNIQUE DESTINY

Stop for a moment to consider this truth: Nobody can praise God exactly the way you do, because no one else has had exactly your experiences; no one has known God's presence and power in the same way you have. Nobody else will use the same combination of words and phrases to express their praise to God. No one else will ever express the same praise in the same way to our great God. Your praise is a unique expression, reflecting your relationship with the Lord.

"Each of the redeemed shall forever know and praise some one aspect of the divine beauty better than any other creature can," C. S. Lewis wrote. "Why else were individuals created, but that God, loving all infinitely, should love each differently?"[3]

Your praise fulfills part of your distinctive destiny as a uniquely created human being. Your praise to God is rooted in the very reason for your creation and your life on this earth.

What is the purpose of our life? If we were to ask Paul that question, he would surely say again what he declares of God in Scripture: "In love he predestined us to be adopted as his sons through Jesus Christ, in accordance with his pleasure and will— *to the praise of his glorious grace*" (Ephesians 1:4-6).

---

3. C. S. Lewis, *The Problem of Pain* (New York: Macmillan, 1962), 150.

If we were to ask Isaiah, he might remind us that God spoke of His people as "the people I formed for myself *that they may proclaim my praise*" (Isaiah 43:21).

If we were to ask Peter, he might proclaim again that even the purpose of our suffering and trials is that our faith "may be proved genuine and *may result in praise, glory and honor* when Jesus Christ is revealed" (1 Peter 1:7).

And what if we asked Jesus? He might recall for us that day when He entered Jerusalem while a great crowd shouted joyful praises to God: "Blessed is the king who comes in the name of the Lord!" and "Peace in heaven and glory in the highest!" (Luke 19:38). And when the Pharisees admonished Jesus that He should rebuke the people for doing this, Jesus replied, "I tell you…if they keep quiet, *the stones will cry out*" (19:40). Humanity's purpose is to enjoy fellowship with God that results in praise to Him, and if God's people fail to fulfill this purpose, the inanimate rocks will shout praises in their place.

I don't know about you, but I certainly don't want a rock doing my job!

YOUR GUIDE TO GREATER PRAISE

This book is designed as a guide to your unique private worship of God and is intended to introduce you to a deeply significant experience with God as you praise Him every day with the exact praise that only you can offer. It's arranged in a thirty-one-day format to help you establish praise as a regular, daily habit in your life. You'll be guided through praise in its many forms and expressions, including some that you may not have considered before.

Your eyes will be opened to the wonder of the God we praise, and more than ever you will understand in the depths of your being just why He deserves unfailing glory and honor.

Great is the LORD, and greatly to be praised;
And His greatness is unsearchable.
       (Psalm 145:3, NKJV)

Yours, O LORD, is the greatness and the power
    and the glory and the majesty and the splendor…
Now, our God, we give you thanks,
    and praise your glorious name.
       (1 Chronicles 29:11,13)

P A R T   1

THE DYNAMICS OF PRAISE

Enter his gates with thanksgiving
and his courts with praise;
give thanks to him and praise his name.

PSALM 100:4

WITH ALL WE HAVE

A man stood in a midweek prayer meeting and began to pray, "O Lord, I will praise You with the instrument of ten strings." Just about everybody in the room opened at least one eye, because we knew there were no musical instruments around. I could sense a feeling of bewilderment throughout the prayer group. How was this man going to praise the Lord with a ten-stringed instrument?

He continued his prayer.

"I will praise You with my *two eyes*—I will look only to You.

"I will praise You by exalting You with my *two ears*—I will listen only to Your voice.

"I will extol You with the work of my *two hands*—I will work in Your service wherever You direct.

"I will honor You with my *two feet*—I will walk in Your statutes, and I will go wherever You lead.

"I will magnify Your holy name with *my tongue*—I will testify constantly to Your loving-kindness.

"I will worship You with *my heart*—I will love only You, and I will receive all the unconditional love You pour out in Your mercy, grace, and forgiveness.

"I thank You, Lord, for the ten-stringed instrument that You built into my being. Keep me in tune and play upon me as You will. Ring out the melodies of Your grace. May the harmony of my praise song bring pleasure to You and glory to Your name. Amen."

This man knew about praising God with everything that was within him. We are to praise the Lord with our minds, offer praise from our hearts, and voice praise with our mouths. Praise involves the use of *all* that we have for God's glory. With everything that is within us, let us praise the Lord!

———◆———

O Lord my God, my deepest desire is to praise You and to love You with all my heart, all my soul, all my mind, all my strength. I express that praise to You now in the words of Your holy Scriptures. Mark 12:30

With David I say, "I will praise you, O Lord my God, with all my heart; I will glorify your name forever." "With

my mouth I will greatly extol the LORD." "In your name
I will lift up my hands." With my ears, "Let me hear
joy and gladness," and praise You for what I hear. With
my eyes, "I will see the goodness of the LORD in the land
of the living," and I will praise You for what I see.
Psalms 86:12; 109:30; 63:4; 51:8; 27:13

IN THE STORM

I grew up in Egypt under the influence of a Christian family. I often sang songs of praise to God, and I would hear my mother and my grandfather praise God for hours at a time. I became a believer in Jesus Christ as a young man, but still I didn't begin to grasp the true meaning of praise until the spring of 1990.

That's when my lovely wife, Elizabeth, was diagnosed with cancer. She was barely forty years old.

My first thought was, *Lord, she's too young to have breast cancer! How can this be happening?* My emotional protest against God was a way of dealing with my fear. I had trouble praying without being overwhelmed with worry over what might happen. I had trouble sleeping, lying awake in bed with a troubled heart. But in the midst of the terrible fear that I might lose my beloved wife, and the frustration that I could not take her place or do anything to protect her except to pray for her, I began to truly learn the power of praise.

Our church was only three years old at the time, and our congregation was still small. But we immediately committed ourselves to intercession. We entered God's course of instruction, Power of Praise 101, with the Holy Spirit and the Bible as our instructors. God began to take me and my family and our church through the first stages of learning what it means to praise Him while standing in the full force of the storm. The more we praised God, the stronger our belief grew that He is capable of all things. His heart breaks with the very same things that force us to our knees. And He is infinitely compassionate toward His hurting and needy children.

We learned a lasting lesson during the time that my wife was battling cancer. The more we praised God, the deeper the fellowship we experienced with Him. As my wife underwent medical treatment that slowly brought physical healing, we underwent spiritual treatment that brought wholeness, hope, strength, and power to our souls. Our spiritual wholeness, and our experience of God's power, came about through praising Him. Our fear over my wife's illness gave way to greater faith in God's rule over our circumstances. Praise fully established the reign of God in our lives.

Ultimately, praise reinforces the truth of who we are and who God is. He alone is the One who makes us whole. He alone is the

One who walks through the dark valley with us. Our faithful Lord never leaves us nor forsakes us. He alone is the Source of all good things.

Praise the Lord! My wife today is in excellent health. We continue to praise God not only for her healing but also for teaching us what it means to be empowered by praise to face any terror, any threat, and any problem that life may hand us.

———◆———

I praise You for Your power, almighty God. "Ah, Sovereign LORD, you have made the heavens and the earth by your great power and outstretched arm. Nothing is too hard for you." With Your Son, Jesus, I say, "Abba, Father…everything is possible for you." Jeremiah 32:17; Mark 14:36

You are the One "who is able to do immeasurably more than all we ask or imagine," according to Your power at work within us. Ephesians 3:20

UNABLE TO HOLD BACK

The Scriptures tell us that our lips reveal whatever we treasure in our hearts. Jesus said, "For where your treasure is, there your heart will be also," and "For out of the overflow of the heart the mouth speaks" (Matthew 6:21; 12:34). Ultimately, we cannot separate what we say and do from what we think and believe deep inside.

If we truly believe in God's love and goodness, that belief will spill over into what we say about Him. No matter what our circumstances, we won't be able to hold back our praise. Do we truly believe that God is the almighty King of the universe and the Lord of our lives? The strength and fervor, the depth and energy of our praise to God—both with our lips and in our lives—is directly proportional to our belief in God's goodness and greatness.

Believing and praising build on each other. The more deeply and strongly we believe, the greater and more expansive is our praise. The more we praise the Lord, the more we will behold His glory and see His hand continually at work in our lives, and the more fervently and strongly we will believe.

Never is this truth put to the test as it is when a dear loved one is in danger. Such a time came when my wife was diagnosed with cancer. It so happened that another person very close to me was gravely ill at the same time. To see two people I loved dearly facing the unknown, possibly even the threat of death itself, tested my beliefs about God. Was He really a God of love, of healing, and of faithfulness? Or was He unconcerned about my family's health and safety?

For most of my life, I had believed the former: That God, in His faithfulness, loves us and cares for us and brings healing. So I started praising Him in advance for His care, His comfort, and His power to heal. In praising Him, I grew to sense in my soul that God truly is who He says He is. God really is the loving Father who comforts us in our time of deepest desperation, fear, and helplessness. Before I knew the final outcome of these threats to my family members' health, I knew without question that God loves us without limit and that He heals us by His power. My life changed from the obedience of duty to the joyful, visceral obedience that expresses itself in uninhibited praise to our loving and all-powerful Lord.

———◆———

My Savior Jesus, I praise You as the Author and Perfecter of my faith. I do believe, because You have helped me to overcome my unbelief. Hebrews 12:2; Mark 9:24

I praise You, God my Father: "In you I trust, O my God." "I trust in your unfailing love; my heart rejoices in your salvation." "I trust in your word." "In God, whose word I praise, in God I trust; I will not be afraid." Psalms 25:2; 13:5; 119:42; 56:4

"I trust in you, O LORD; I say, 'You are my God.'" Psalm 31:14

CHOOSING TO PRAISE

The world hassles us every day; I don't have to tell you that. Our fears, anxieties, and hurts are very real. But if we focus only on these earthly problems, then very soon the spiritual realm becomes foggy and unreal. We lose sight of God and slide into pessimism and even depression. Life loses its joy and excitement. If we limit our thinking to this world alone, it will grind us down into the dust from which we were created.

No matter how difficult or unjust our circumstances become, we can exercise our free will and choose to praise God rather than ignore Him. We can choose not only *what* we will praise Him for, but how long, how frequently, and how intensely we will praise Him.

Praise has a strong emotional dimension—as we see in the psalms—but it isn't driven by emotions. Praise is driven by our will. That's why we must never say, "I prefer to wait and praise God when I really feel like it." We're to praise God in *all* situations, in both victory and defeat, when we're in need and when we're experiencing plenty.

In fact, the times when you *don't* feel like praising God are precisely the moments when it's most essential to do so. The next time you're discouraged, start praising God. When you feel defeated or unable to break loose from bad habits, start praising God. When your most treasured relationships seem to be falling apart, start praising God.

Why do I say this? Because praise is about what God desires us to do—it's not about the power of your circumstances. When you get your eyes off your immediate problem and put your focus on God, you redirect yourself toward what God will do for you, not what man has done to you. At that point, God can work in your life to produce real growth.

The truth for the believer is that this tangible, physical world is not the "real" world. The real world is our *ultimate* home—the heavenly, spiritual realm where God's presence permeates the atmosphere. When we start to view our present life in light of this ultimate reality, things begin to change. Faith and hope take root and flourish; joy and peace grow in our hearts.

This is how praise alters our feelings. Praise focuses our attention on the world of the Spirit, the heavenly, spiritual reality where He calls us to live and move. Praise brings joy to adverse circumstances.

———◆———

I make my choice this day to praise and to serve You, O God, my Master. "As for me and my household, we will serve the LORD." Joshua 24:15

And I choose to serve and praise You for the rest of my life on earth and for eternity. "I will exalt you, my God the King; I will praise your name for ever and ever. Every day I will praise you and extol your name for ever and ever." Psalm 145:1-2

"I desire to do your will, O my God; your law is within my heart." "Your kingdom come, your will be done on earth as it is in heaven." Psalm 40:8; Matthew 6:10

WHERE GOD CAMPS

Through praise we experience more fully God's presence, both within us and at work all around us. The Scriptures tell us that God dwells in the praises of His people. He is the holy God "that inhabitest the praises of Israel" (Psalm 22:3, KJV). The image painted by the psalmist is that God sits down and takes delight in the praises offered to His name. God pitches His tent wherever His name is exalted. He camps out with those who acknowledge, glorify, and desire His presence.

If you're struggling with pain, sickness, or loss and are desperate for a sense of God's nearness, then start praising His holy name. As my wife and I recoiled at the surgeon's word *cancer,* we clung to God in praise of His love, His protection, and His faithfulness. We needed Him to set up camp amid our weakness and fear and suffering. And He did!

The simple fact of God's presence is this: Wherever God dwells, God rules. He is our authority. When we invite God to dwell in us, He reigns over our hearts. When we invite God to dwell in our marriages and our family relationships, God reigns over those relationships. When we invite God to exert His will and presence in our business, He reigns over our business.

Praise is our foremost means of inviting God to take up His residence with us and to establish His presence, authority, and purpose in every area of our lives. As we praise our Lord, we enjoy the warmest, deepest form of fellowship with our heavenly Father. No matter what you're facing, praise Him now.

———◆———

"I love the house where you live, O LORD, the place where your glory dwells." I love You for coming to dwell within me and for making my heart Your home. Because You have done this, "Therefore my heart is glad and my tongue rejoices." I am "filled with an inexpressible and glorious joy." Psalms 26:8; 16:9; 1 Peter 1:8

Because You dwell within me, "My heart says of you, 'Seek his face!' Your face, LORD, I will seek." Psalm 27:8

THE TRUTH ABOUT GOD
AND ABOUT US

An amazing thing happens as we praise God for all He is and does. We see more clearly the truth of His nature. We see that He is the unlimited, holy, eternal King. We see that He is all-knowing, all-wise, and all-powerful. We see Him as loving, merciful, and long-suffering.

When we come to God in praise and adoration, we also see more clearly the truth about ourselves, including the truth of our sinfulness and unworthiness. Let me openly confess that I've never come into the presence of God—praising Him, adoring Him, and honoring Him with the fruit of my lips—when I did not also become more conscious of my own limitations, faults, and sins.

The more we grasp all that God is, the more we face all that we are not.

Job was a man so godly that God bragged about him, but when God revealed His great power, Job replied in humility,

> I know that you can do all things;
>   no plan of yours can be thwarted....
> My ears had heard of you
>   but now my eyes have seen you.
> Therefore I despise myself
>   and repent in dust and ashes.
>   (Job 42:2,5-6)

No matter how righteous we are, seeing God's glory confronts us with the tarnish and stain of our own lives. The reason for this is not to make us walk through life with our heads hanging low but that we might repent of our sin and rely on God and cry out to Him to forgive us and to strengthen us by the power of His Holy Spirit.

Praise God because He gives us an opportunity to see our sin so we can ask Him to work in us, to change us into the men and women we truly desire to become. The prayer of our hearts should always be "God, make me into the person You want to live with forever!"

———◆———

Holy God, as I learn about who You are, "my soul will rejoice in the LORD and delight in his salvation. My whole being will exclaim, 'Who is like you, O LORD?' " "I will give thanks to the LORD because of his righteousness and will sing praise to the name of the LORD Most High." Psalms 35:9-10; 7:17

"Let me live that I may praise you." Psalm 119:175

"I will praise you, O Lord my God, with all my heart; I will glorify your name forever." Psalm 86:12

FOR THE JOY

When I was a boy growing up in Egypt, my grandfather was a building contractor by trade and a lay leader in the Brethren Church. He lived in a small apartment adjacent to the home of my cousins, and when I spent the night with them, I'd find myself waking up several times during the night. From his apartment next door I would hear my grandfather praising the Lord. He seemed to praise God around the clock or at least several times a night.

My grandfather lost two sons when they were in their early thirties, and he lost his wife while he was still a relatively young man, but he was always full of joy. Praise gave my grandfather his joyful heart. Until he died at the age of ninety-two, he never ceased to praise God throughout the night and then again in the morning.

My mother had grown up with this man's model of devotion to God, and it shaped her life. It wasn't unusual for her to pray for one or two hours at a time. She had developed this spiritual discipline of prayer and praise from observing her father. Nothing the world offers could ever compare with this rich spiritual legacy that I inherited from my mother and grandfather.

Why should we praise God? Perhaps the foremost reason is the one evident in the life of my grandfather: joy. We praise God as an expression of our joy in Him, and that praise in turn produces in us a life of deep and abiding joy.

You can't read the book of Revelation without realizing that the joy of praise forms the atmosphere of heaven. What an unspeakably glorious praise song is filling heaven this very minute. I have no doubt that my grandfather and mother are part of that great praise choir! What joy to know that we who are in Christ Jesus will be praising God and adoring Him forever. Our bodies may be buried on this earth, but our praise will never die. It will go on forever.

———◆———

"I will be glad and rejoice in you; I will sing praise to your name, O Most High." "My soul will rejoice in the LORD and delight in his salvation." Psalms 9:2; 35:9

"You have made known to me the path of life; you will fill me with joy in your presence, with eternal pleasures at your right hand." Psalm 16:11

Yes, Father, this is true for me: "The LORD has done great things for us, and we are filled with joy." "Let the heavens rejoice, let the earth be glad." Psalm 126:3; 96:11

THE HOPE THAT ENERGIZES

Have you ever been so discouraged that you couldn't sleep? Have you ever been so worn out by life's troubles that you couldn't rest? Weariness of the soul exhausts us. To those who know this exhaustion, God offers a hope that energizes us:

> Do you not know?
>> Have you not heard?
> The LORD is the everlasting God,
>> the Creator of the ends of the earth.
> He will not grow tired or weary,
>> and his understanding no one can fathom.

He gives strength to the weary
and increases the power of the weak.
Even youths grow tired and weary,
and young men stumble and fall;
but those who hope in the LORD
will renew their strength.
They will soar on wings like eagles;
they will run and not grow weary,
they will walk and not be faint.
(Isaiah 40:28-31)

The prophet Isaiah told us that those who hope in the Lord have their strength renewed and their energy restored. But how do we acquire this hope?

We become hopeful when we look at what God can do, not at what man has done. Hope wells up in us when we focus on the capabilities of God, not the weakness and inability of man. Hope springs up when we praise God for His perfection—recognizing and acknowledging and trusting in all that He is—rather than giving honor to the feeble attempts and less-than-perfect accomplishments of man.

If you're exhausted at the end of the day, shut yourself in for a while with God. Praise Him with every ounce of energy that remains in you. You'll be refreshed, not only mentally and emotionally, but physically. There's a special strength that is imparted to those who praise the Lord. This kind of strength gives you the power of hope to endure, to persevere, to outlast tough times. It gives you the power to intercede until God gives a breakthrough.

I am 100 percent convinced that the best medicine for spiritual exhaustion is praise.

———◆———

I praise You, Almighty God, for Your energizing power.
"Be exalted, O LORD, in your strength." Psalm 21:13

I praise You for Your energy that You have caused to flow through me. "It is God who arms me with strength and makes my way perfect. He makes my feet like the feet of a deer; he enables me to stand on the heights." Because of the energy You supply, "I run in the path of your commands." Psalms 18:32-33; 119:32

Because all this is true, I "sing and praise your might." Psalm 21:13

SEEING GOD FOR WHO HE IS

Your view of God determines your praise, and your praise mirrors your view of God.

If you believe that He is your loving, patient, and forgiving heavenly Father, your praise will reflect those qualities of God.

If you believe that God cares about you every moment and in every circumstance and that no situation is beyond His notice and His care, then you're likely to be praising God all the time! "Praise the Lord" will be something you say in one form or another countless times throughout the day.

If you're deeply grateful that God has saved you from the consequences of your sin, you'll have so much praise that you cannot express it all in just a few moments. Your praise will be overflowing because your gratitude is so great.

If you see God as fully willing to move heaven and earth on your behalf, your praise will be enthusiastic and heartfelt! Those who see God as being on their side, working always for their eternal benefit, are those who praise God with the most intensity and the greatest amount of faith.

God's greatness can leave us speechless in awe. His greatness can easily make the language of praise more difficult, but it also makes praise necessary. Praise brings us to a fuller recognition of God—not so that we might cower before Him, but so that we might bow before Him in humble worship. We worship God not so much to do something for Him, although He does desire our praise, but we worship Him to affirm His lordship over our lives.

The word *worship* comes from the word *worth-ship,* which means expressing to God His worth to us. How much do you value who God is? How much do you value what God has done for you? How much do you rely daily on what God promises to do for you? How much worth do you place on your relationship with Him?

———◆———

O Lord, You are infinitely good. You are infinitely great.
   With full faith I confess this beautiful truth: "The LORD
is good to all; he has compassion on all he has made." Your

"compassions never fail. They are new every morning; great is your faithfulness." Psalm 145:9; Lamentations 3:22-23

And I exalt Your greatness: "How great are your works, O LORD, how profound your thoughts!" "Praise the LORD, O my soul. O LORD my God, you are very great; you are clothed with splendor and majesty." Psalms 92:5; 104:1

SPIRITUALLY OPEN

Praise opens our eyes and ears to God. When we focus on the Lord in praise, we're much more likely to hear what He has to say to us. Praise opens us up spiritually to hear God's commands.

In fact, that truth helps explain why praise is often so difficult for us: Praise demands that we make changes in our lives, and most of us don't welcome the prospect of change. It takes courage to reexamine what we believe to be true about ourselves and about God and to realize what we need to change about our lives.

Sometimes the change God commands will require us to confess and repent of a sin and to make adjustments in how we live, especially in how we think of others and relate to others. We cannot harbor anger, resentment, or hatred toward others and at the same time genuinely praise God. A negative spirit toward others and positive praise to God simply cannot coexist.

Oh, you may begin your praise out of a sense of duty. You may come to God only out of obedience and begin praising Him without having a completely thankful heart. But once you start praising God, you cannot continue for long without that negative spirit being broken. I have seen this happen over and over again in my own life. No matter how bleak or sad my circumstances, I am uplifted as I praise the Lord. As I honor God for who He is and for the glorious things He has done, my eyes are opened to God's abundant provision and blessing.

Sometimes God's command compels us to move to a deeper level of commitment or to move out in a closer walk of faith. Whatever He wants to tell us, it will be easier to hear Him clearly when we're praising Him.

———◆———

"O great and powerful God, whose name is the LORD Almighty, great are your purposes and mighty are your deeds. Your eyes are open to all the ways of men; you reward everyone according to his conduct and as his deeds deserve." Jeremiah 32:18-19

"Your righteousness is like the mighty mountains, your justice like the great deep." "Your righteousness is everlasting and your law is true." Psalms 36:6; 119:142

"The earth is filled with your love, O LORD; teach me your decrees." Psalm 119:64

WITH A SINCERE HEART

Pride is deadly, which is why we need the healing and protection that come through the praise of our Lord. Praise reveals pride for the spiritual disease that it is. Either pride will stop the flow of praise from a person's lips, or praise will uproot and defeat pride.

But pride isn't the only sin that kills praise. An untrue heart—insincere, hypocritical, or filled with doubt—can also squelch both our desire and our ability to praise God.

Hebrews 10:22 tells us, "Let us draw near to God *with a sincere heart* in full assurance of faith." We may try to draw near to God with our words, yet restrain our heart from genuine intimacy with our heavenly Father because of harbored doubt or bitterness or anger or even a determination to continue living in some type of disobedience.

It's possible to fool others and even to fool ourselves when it comes to praise, but it's never possible to fool God. He knows the intent, motives, and desires of our heart. For praise to be acceptable to almighty God, our heart must be true. And when the Bible speaks of the heart, it means the totality of our inner being—the intricate combination of intellect, emotional response, and will. All three of these must line up with God's perfect will.

You may think, *Well, then, I don't have a chance! My intellect, emotions, and will often move in the very opposite direction from God's plan.* My friend, don't be dismayed. God never intended for you to conform to His will on your own. That's why He sent His Holy Spirit to give you the grace and power to live a righteous life. That's the very essence of His grace.

God has never made a demand on us that He hasn't covered by His own provision. His Holy Spirit nudges, prods, molds, and fashions us so that our heart is true—so that our thoughts line up with our words, our words line up with our behavior, and our motives and plans line up with God's desires.

———◆———

I lift my voice to "praise and exalt and glorify the King of heaven, because everything he does is right and all his ways

are just. And those who walk in pride he is able to humble.”
Daniel 4:37

"I will praise you, O Lord, with all my heart.” Psalm 9:1

"I have set the Lord always before me. Because he is at my right hand, I will not be shaken. Therefore my heart is glad and my tongue rejoices.” Psalm 16:8-9

FULL SURRENDER

In Genesis 22 we find a wonderful picture of a believer's total submission to God. It's the account of Abraham's response when the Lord commanded him to offer his son Isaac as a burnt offering.

Abraham submitted his intellect when he obeyed this command. He surrendered his heart and his feelings as well. For Abraham to bind his son to an altar and to raise a knife against him must have been the greatest emotional agony a human could know. Most of all we see Abraham's surrender of his will. He followed God's will, not his own, because he fully expected God to raise Isaac from the dead. Abraham knew that the Lord would stand by His promise to bless the earth through Isaac.

The decision to surrender all of your life before God is a solitary, individual decision. You are the only one who can yield your all to Christ. Abraham did not even tell his wife, Sarah, what God had commanded. I have wondered what I would do in such a situation. Would I be willing to obey without first gathering Christian brothers around me to offer their prayers and advice? I feel certain that if Abraham had consulted anyone else, he would have been told, in so many words, "Abe, you're not thinking clearly. Surely God doesn't want you to do this. You're hearing a voice, all right, but it's not God's."

I am not at all suggesting that it is wrong to get godly counsel. But in the end, we personally are responsible for surrendering fully to God. We must obey as He directs us. God expects our surrender to be total, to be daily, and to be a sacrifice.

Praise costs us something—our pride and our self-serving plans. Praise requires that we lay ourselves down on an altar before the Lord and say, "I yield to You every aspect of my life—all my talent, all my possessions, all my dreams, all my relationships."

I encourage you to pray this prayer today:

Lord Jesus,
    I surrender my intellect,
    I surrender my emotions,
    I surrender my will.

Lord Jesus,
    Help me to surrender daily.
    Help me to obey You daily,
    that I may worship You with a true heart.
    Amen.

———◆———

"I will sacrifice a freewill offering to you; I will praise your name, O LORD, for it is good." Psalm 54:6

"I trust in the LORD. I will be glad and rejoice in your love…. I trust in you, O LORD; I say, 'You are my God.' My times are in your hands." Psalm 31:6-7,14-15

"I will say of the LORD, 'He is my refuge and my fortress, my God, in whom I trust.'" Psalm 91:2

"I trust in your word." Psalm 119:42

PART II

THE GOD WE PRAISE

Sing the glory of his name;
make his praise glorious!

PSALM 66:2

PRAISE HIS NAME

Praise the *name* of the Lord! Throughout the psalms we read this admonition, and we hear it frequently in the church as well. But what does it mean to praise the Lord's name? Shouldn't we concentrate instead on what God does?

The names of God that are revealed in Scripture are not a human invention. They are the way in which God has chosen to reveal His character to us. The names of God are a composite of God's revelation of His nature, His identity, His sovereignty, and His desires. If you want to know God, get to know His names. The names of God are evidence that He desires for us to know Him intimately, to praise Him more completely, and to enter more fully into a deep and abiding relationship with Him.

Confessing God's name is a form of sacrifice. Many churches on Sunday morning sing an upbeat Scripture chorus that speaks of bringing "the sacrifice of praise" into the house of the Lord. Many who sing this song might wonder just what it means. We find the answer in Hebrews 13:15: "Through Jesus, therefore, let us continually offer to God a sacrifice of praise—the fruit of lips that *confess his name.*" A sacrifice of praise is the confession of the names of the Lord—it is speaking His name in relationship to our personal life.

When we praise the Lord using the names of God, we are praising the Trinity, the full Godhead, because God's Old Testament names are not reserved only for the Father. They reveal the nature of the triune God—Father, Son, and Holy Spirit. When we praise God with these names, we're praising Him in His fullness.

As we praise God for all that His names mean, we must also remember what an incomparable privilege it is to be an adopted child of such an awesome God. Because we're His children, God has sent His Holy Spirit into our hearts. The Spirit enables us to use the intimate and tender name for our heavenly Father: *Abba*—Daddy God. We are the children of our loving Father, and as His children, we are also His heirs (Galatians 4:6-7).

———◆———

"I will sing praise to your name, O Most High." "How awesome is the LORD *Most High, the great King over all the earth!" Yes, Lord, how awesome You are!* Psalms 9:2; 47:2

"Like your name, O God, your praise reaches to the ends of the earth." Psalm 48:10

"In your name I will hope, for your name is good."
"O LORD, our Lord, how majestic is your name in all the earth!" Psalms 52:9; 8:1

"Great is the LORD, and most worthy of praise."
Psalm 48:1

ELOHIM, THE MOST HIGH GOD

The first name God revealed to humanity was Elohim, a name that appears more than twenty-five hundred times throughout the Old Testament. God's people knew that this name referred to the "most high" God or the "highest" God—the God above all creation, the God who initiated and created all of life.

Living all around God's people were pagans who worshiped gods they had fashioned and defined according to human standards. To declare that there was only one God and that He reigned supreme over the entire universe was a radically different concept.

When God's people encountered nations who worshiped Baal, the god of fertility, the Hebrews responded, "We worship

Elohim, the One who authorizes the birth of children." When they encountered pagans who worshiped the god Shamish, the sun god, the Hebrews responded, "We worship Elohim. He is the One who put the sun in its place and who governs its course."

Elohim, the God of all creation, includes all three persons of the Trinity. We know that Jesus was present at Creation. As John writes: "In the beginning was the Word, and the Word was with God, and the Word was God. He was with God in the beginning. Through him all things were made; without him nothing was made that has been made" (John 1:1-3).

We know also that the Holy Spirit was present at creation: "The Spirit of God was hovering over the waters" (Genesis 1:2). God the Holy Spirit has been "moving" and "hovering" over life ever since. He is the Creator of all "newness of life" that we experience in Christ Jesus.

Praise Elohim! He is the one true and living God. He alone is God. He is the Creator of each new day in our life, each new experience we encounter, and each new spiritual work in us. He is the Author and Finisher of our faith.

———◆———

I praise You, Elohim, as "the great God, the great King above all gods." "Great is the LORD and most worthy of praise; he is to be feared above all gods." Psalms 95:3; 96:4

"I know that the LORD is great, that our Lord is greater than all gods. The LORD does whatever pleases him, in the

heavens and on the earth, in the seas and all their depths."
For this I praise and exalt You, Most High God. Psalm 135:5-6

"How great is your goodness, which you have stored up
for those who fear you, which you bestow in the sight of men
on those who take refuge in you." Psalm 31:19

EL-SHADDAI, GOD ALMIGHTY

To Abraham, who was then called Abram, God revealed more of His nature when He revealed another of His names, El-Shaddai. This name means "God of power and might." El-Shaddai is the all-powerful, all-sufficient God. El-Shaddai is God Almighty.

This name reveals a God who controls and subdues nature. El-Shaddai is the God to whom all nature listens and obeys.

Nearly every time God expresses Himself to someone as El-Shaddai, He indicates a change that will occur in that person's life, a change that will involve a miraculous intervention.

God said to Abram: "I am God Almighty [El-Shaddai]; walk before me and be blameless. I will confirm my covenant between me and you and will greatly increase your numbers" (Genesis

17:1-2). As soon as God revealed this name, Abram fell facedown before Him. God told Abram that he would have many descendants and that his name would be changed to Abraham, which means "father of many nations." God was going to intervene and use His power to cause Abraham to father a son, even though Abraham's wife, Sarai, was barren.

God later used this same divine name when He revealed Himself to Jacob, saying, "I am God Almighty [El-Shaddai].... A nation and a community of nations will come from you, and kings will come from your body. The land I gave to Abraham and Isaac I also give to you, and...to your descendants after you" (Genesis 35:11-12). At the time God spoke these words, Jacob had lost his son Joseph and did not know he was still alive in Egypt. Jacob's sons Simeon and Levi had caused tremendous problems with the pagan tribes that inhabited the land. God was saying to Jacob, in essence, "I am going to intervene on your behalf. You will become a great nation, and you will receive this land that I have promised to you. I am the Lord Almighty—the course of nature and the course of history run according to My plans."

God wants there to be no misunderstanding—as El-Shaddai, He is the Ruler and Owner of all things. He is the controlling force of all nature and all history.

———◆———

"O Lord, open my lips, and my mouth will declare your praise." Psalm 51:15

"O my Strength, I sing praise to you; you, O God, are my fortress, my loving God." "In God, whose word I praise, in God I trust; I will not be afraid." Psalms 59:17; 56:4

"The LORD lives! Praise be to my Rock! Exalted be God my Savior!" "The glory of the LORD is great." Psalms 18:46; 138:5

"I will praise you forever for what you have done." Psalm 52:9

El-Shaddai
Calms Our Storms

One evening after a long day of ministry, Jesus and His disciples were crossing the Sea of Galilee in a small boat, and a great storm arose. They were in danger of capsizing when the disciples finally awoke Jesus, who was calmly asleep. "Teacher," they cried, "don't you care if we drown?" (Mark 4:38).

Jesus arose, rebuked the wind, and said to the waves, "Quiet! Be still!" (verse 39). The wind died down immediately, and the sea became calm. The disciples were awestruck and said to one another, "Who is this? Even the wind and the waves obey him!" (verse 41).

Who is this? The answer is that Jesus is El-Shaddai—God Almighty, God who governs the winds and the waves and fulfills His plan on the earth.

This miracle of Jesus' calming the sea was a real-life manifestation of a scene in Psalm 107 describing the power of God Almighty in delivering those who "went out on the sea in ships" (verse 23):

> He stilled the storm to a whisper;
>> the waves of the sea were hushed.
> They were glad when it grew calm,
>> and he guided them to their desired haven.
>> (verses 29-30)

Do you need God to calm a storm in your life? Do you need healing that He alone can give? Then cry out to El-Shaddai. Begin to praise God Almighty! He alone can hold you up when all seems to be crumbling around you. He alone can ride the clouds to bring help for you. He alone can open doors that no one can shut and shut doors that no one else can open.

We make a great mistake when we attempt to do things in our own strength. El-Shaddai desires to manifest Himself as God Almighty on our behalf.

Praise El-Shaddai today! He is at work inside your heart. He desires to change you, to change conditions around you, and ultimately to change the entire world.

———◆———

"Mightier than the thunder of the great waters, mightier than the breakers of the sea—the LORD on high is mighty." Psalm 93:4

"I will exalt you, O LORD, for you lifted me out of the depths." "You are God my Savior, and my hope is in you all day long." Psalms 30:1; 25:5

"O LORD, you are my God; I will exalt you and praise your name, for in perfect faithfulness you have done marvelous things, things planned long ago." Isaiah 25:1

JEHOVAH-JIREH, GOD OUR PROVIDER

Jehovah is an English rendition of the Hebrew *Yahweh,* the name for God that is used in the Old Testament more than any other—more than sixty-eight hundred times (in English Bibles it's usually translated as "the LORD"). This name literally means "to be." It has been translated as "The Ever-Living One" and "The Self-Existing One." Our God depends upon nothing and no one for His existence.

One of the foremost variations of this name is Jehovah-Jireh, which means "the Lord will provide." It's the name Abraham used for the place on the mountain where God had sent him to sacrifice his beloved son, Isaac, as a burnt offering (see Genesis 22).

On the way up this mountain, Isaac said to his father, " 'The fire and wood are here...but where is the lamb for the burnt offering?' Abraham answered, 'God himself will provide the lamb for the burnt offering, my son' " (22:7-8).

After Abraham bound his son, laid him on the altar, and raised his knife to slay him, an angel of the Lord called to him: "Do not lay a hand on the boy.... Now I know that you fear God, because you have not withheld from me your son, your only son" (22:12). Then Abraham saw a ram caught by its horns in a nearby thicket. He took the ram and sacrificed it in place of his son. And he called that place Jehovah-Jireh, "The LORD Will Provide" (22:14).

The word *jireh* literally means "he sees ahead." God sees what we need even before we realize we need it. For every task God gives you, He has already made full provision for all you'll need to complete it. There's no troublesome circumstance or difficulty for which He hasn't already provided your victory or a way of escape. There's nothing you face today or in the future that God hasn't already foreseen and arranged everything you'll need to equip you to face it.

Praise Jehovah-Jireh! God is our provider today, tomorrow, and for eternity. Praise our God who sees ahead and already has a plan to provide everything we'll ever need!

———◆———

This is my reminder: "Praise the LORD, O my soul, and forget not all his benefits—who forgives all your sins and heals all your diseases, who redeems your life from the pit and crowns you with love and compassion, who satisfies your desires with good things so that your youth is renewed like the eagle's." Psalm 103:2-5

Yes, Lord, You are the One who "satisfies the thirsty and fills the hungry with good things." "You are great and do marvelous deeds; you alone are God." Psalms 107:9; 86:10

JEHOVAH-RAPHA, GOD OUR HEALER

In Exodus 15:26, God makes this promise to His people: "If you listen carefully to the voice of the LORD your God and do what is right in his eyes, if you pay attention to his commands and keep all his decrees, I will not bring on you any of the diseases I brought on the Egyptians, for I am the LORD, who heals you." This last phrase is the name Jehovah-Rapha.

The word *rapha* means to heal and to restore. God doesn't promise to heal us only in isolated instances. Rather, God says He *is* healing. He is our wholeness. He is what we ultimately need, no matter what weakness or sickness or trouble we encounter.

We see this truth echoed in the New Testament every time Jesus commands someone to be healed or made whole. Wholeness is God's desire for us. No disease, nothing that causes us pain or suffering, can withstand the healing touch of Jesus.

Does this mean God isn't true to His name if a believer becomes ill or is suffering from a terminal disease? Not at all. That believer can be assured that God desires to use this suffering to bring an even greater reward of healing to that person and to bring an even greater awareness of His healing presence to others who may witness the person's steadfastness.

All of us will die someday, but God tells us He will never forsake us, not even in death. He's with us always, working all things to our eternal good. In the moment of our death, God seals the wholeness issue and we truly are "made whole" for all eternity.

The ongoing work of the Holy Spirit in our world is the work of Jehovah-Rapha. It's the Holy Spirit who mends broken hearts, renews degenerate minds, restores shattered relationships, and heals disease. It's the work of the Holy Spirit to conform us to the likeness of the perfect, complete Christ Jesus.

Praise Jehovah-Rapha, the God who heals us and makes us whole!

———◆———

"Your compassion is great, O LORD." "Heal me, O LORD, and I will be healed; save me and I will be saved, for you are the one I praise." Psalm 119:156; Jeremiah 17:14

I hear Your promise to the child of Your covenant: "I will heal him; I will guide him and restore comfort to him." Isaiah 57:18

And I hear Your words to those who belong to You: "I will heal my people." "Then your light will break forth like the dawn, and your healing will quickly appear." Jeremiah 33:6; Isaiah 58:8

JEHOVAH-NISSI, GOD OUR BANNER

In Exodus 17 the Amalekites wanted to prevent the people of Israel from continuing their journey toward the Promised Land. So Moses told Joshua, "Choose some of our men and go out to fight the Amalekites. Tomorrow I will stand on top of the hill with the staff of God in my hands" (17:9).

This staff of God that Moses held in his upraised hands the next day was like a battle flag or banner, signaling to everyone the Lord's presence with Israel. "As long as Moses held up his hands," this passage tells us, "the Israelites were winning, but whenever he lowered his hands, the Amalekites were winning" (17:11). When

Moses' hands grew tired, his helpers Aaron and Hur sat him on a stone and held up his hands so they remained steady until sunset. That was enough time for Joshua to overcome the Amalekite army.

After this great victory, "Moses built an altar and called it The LORD is my Banner [Jehovah-Nissi]. He said, 'For hands were lifted up to the throne of the LORD' " (17:15-16).

As Jehovah-Nissi, God raises His miracle-working power over our lives to bring us victory against every enemy of our souls. His "banner" over us is the assurance that we'll move forward to achieve all that He has planned for us.

What enemies do you face today? Do you face a threat from someone who seeks to harm you personally or professionally, to hurt your family or business? Do you face the nagging fear that failure is around the next bend? An enemy can be any form of anxiety that causes a lump in your throat or a feeling of dread in the pit of your stomach—anything that seeks to stop you from proceeding into the fullness of all that God has designated as yours.

These enemies can seem like giants, but giants are nothing when you lift your hands in praise to God and trust Him to be your strong staff of victory. God's ultimate victory is certain.

Praise our God, Jehovah-Nissi, the banner of victory over our lives today!

———◆———

"The LORD's right hand is lifted high; the LORD's right hand has done mighty things!" Psalm 118:16

"I call to the LORD, who is worthy of praise, and I am saved from my enemies." "You give me your shield of victory, and your right hand sustains me; you stoop down to make me great." Psalm 18:3,35

I say with confidence, "For those who fear you, you have raised a banner to be unfurled against the bow." And I rejoice that Your "banner over me is love." Psalm 60:4; Song of Songs 2:4

JEHOVAH-MEKADDISH, GOD WHO MAKES US HOLY

Many people are uncomfortable with the word *holiness*. They think it refers to unreasonable restrictions on their behavior or appearance. The word *holy*, however, means to be cleansed and separated for God's purposes. All Christians are called to be holy. We're called to be cleansed of our sins by the shed blood of Christ, to be sealed for God's purposes by the power of the Holy Spirit, and to live righteous lives for God.

The Hebrew word that means holy or sanctified is *mekaddish*. This term is used to describe people who are set apart for divine callings. In Leviticus 20:7-8, God says, "Consecrate yourselves and be holy, because I am the LORD your God. Keep my decrees and follow them. I am the LORD, who makes you holy"—and this last phrase is the name Jehovah-Mekaddish.

We're made holy not only by being in God's presence but also by having His presence in us. The apostle Paul asked us, "Don't you know that you yourselves are God's temple and that God's Spirit lives in you?… For God's temple is sacred, and you are that temple" (1 Corinthians 3:16-17).

Paul asked again, "Do you not know that your body is a temple of the Holy Spirit, who is in you, whom you have received from God? You are not your own; you were bought at a price. Therefore honor God with your body" (1 Corinthians 6:19-20).

If it was up to us to live a holy life on our own strength or to cleanse our lives by our own efforts, we all would have bombed out long ago. It isn't our own efforts that make us holy, but God's work within us that makes us holy. Living within us, the Holy Spirit sanctifies us. We're holy because God says we're holy, and He makes us holy.

What a tremendous and awesome mystery that we can be made and called holy by a Holy God! Praise God today that He is Jehovah-Mekaddish. He is our holiness!

———◆———

"You are enthroned as the Holy One." "Your ways, O God, are holy." "Great is the Holy One of Israel." "Holiness adorns your house for endless days, O LORD." Psalms 22:3; 77:13; Isaiah 12:6; Psalm 93:5

*In obedience I respond to Your call: "Ascribe to the L*ORD *the glory due his name; worship the L*ORD *in the splendor of his holiness." "I will sing praise to you…O Holy One of Israel."* Psalm 29:2; 71:22

*"Praise the L*ORD, *O my soul; all my inmost being, praise his holy name."* Psalm 103:1

JEHOVAH-SHALOM, GOD OUR PEACE

In Judges 6 a young man named Gideon made an altar for the Lord and called it Jehovah-Shalom, The LORD is Peace (6:24). Why was peace so important to him just at that moment?

The Israelites had been living under the tyranny of the Midianites, who routinely destroyed their crops and took or killed their livestock. The Midianites completely impoverished the Israelites.

The Israelites had forgotten about God, but now they cried out for His help. He responded by sending an angel to speak to Gideon. After Gideon realized who this visitor was, he exclaimed,

"Ah, Sovereign LORD! I have seen the angel of the LORD face to face!" (6:22). Gideon held to the belief of his day that to have a direct encounter with the Lord was to die.

But the Lord said to him, "Peace! Do not be afraid. You are not going to die" (6:23). Still today, those who have a face-to-face encounter with God and yield to His will, bowing before Him in repentance and praise, will be those who *live* not only now but forever.

In response to this visitation from God, Gideon built an altar that he named Jehovah-Shalom. *Shalom,* the Hebrew word for peace, means far more than an absence of conflict or an emotional feeling of contentment. *Shalom* means perfect well-being. It means to be filled with a perfect peace, a comprehensive peace, a peace that surpasses our understanding.

The only way to experience this unwavering peace is to know with certainty that God has met us, forgiven us, received us, and given us the gift of eternal life. Jesus doesn't just give us peace; He *is* our peace. What He did for us on the cross enables us to enter into a spiritual rest that is free from guilt, shame, and the fear of death.

Praise the Lord today that He gives a calm to our souls that truly is beyond our understanding (see Philippians 4:7), a peace that cannot be shaken by life's circumstances. He gives us the peace that all is well and that we're destined to enjoy an eternity in the glorious light of His countenance. Praise Jehovah-Shalom!

"LORD, you establish peace for us; all that we have accomplished you have done for us." Isaiah 26:12

I praise You, Lord Jesus, as Jehovah-Shalom, for You Yourself are our peace. You are "the Prince of Peace," and of Your government and peace "there will be no end." Ephesians 2:14; Isaiah 9:6-7

This I know is true: "The LORD blesses his people with peace." "I will lie down and sleep in peace, for you alone, O LORD, make me dwell in safety." Psalms 29:11; 4:8

JEHOVAH-ROHI, GOD OUR SHEPHERD

One of the most beautiful images of God in all the Bible is that of a shepherd leading, protecting, and caring for his sheep. *Rohi* is the Hebrew word for shepherd, and there's no more tender word to describe the relationship between God and His people. This is the picture of God we see in Psalm 23, which begins, "The LORD is my shepherd, I shall not be in want."

From the riches of this familiar psalm, we can find endless ways to praise God our Shepherd. He provides for all our needs so we're never in want. Just as a shepherd leads his sheep to pasture, so the Lord leads us into places of abundant nourishment and rest, into times of spiritual refreshment and retreat.

Like a shepherd, He guides us into right choices and decisions, right beliefs, right words, and right actions, so that all of our life brings glory to His name. We can praise the Lord because, as our Shepherd, He has given us His Word, the Bible, and also His Holy Spirit to show us the way to live and to affirm that we're His forever. He rescues us anytime we fall away from the path that is right.

Like a shepherd, He is with us in times of danger. He never leaves us, and He drives fear from us. He gives us His joy even when we're being persecuted by others. We can praise Him that He has prepared an eternal home for us so that we'll never be separated from Him.

God's assurance banishes all fears, and He enables us to do great works in His name. We can praise Him because He's always at work to conform us to the likeness of Christ Jesus and because His desire is for us to walk daily in His tender care so that we can always say, "Surely goodness and love will follow me all the days of my life, and I will dwell in the house of the LORD forever" (Psalm 23:6).

Praise the Lord that He is our Shepherd, Jehovah-Rohi!

———————◆———————

O God, I thank You for Your tender Shepherd's love shown for me.

I praise You, loving Father, because Your Word says that You're a shepherd who "gathers the lambs in his arms and carries them close to his heart." Isaiah 40:11

I praise You, Lord Jesus, for being our Good Shepherd who "lays down his life for the sheep." John 10:11

I praise You, Holy Spirit, for Your shepherdlike care in giving us faithful counsel, trustworthy conviction, and comforting presence. John 14:26; 16:7-11; 14:16

JEHOVAH-TSIDKENU, GOD OUR RIGHTEOUSNESS

In the days of King Josiah, God's people had been living in sin and idolatry, and their land was oppressed on all sides by violence and crime. King Josiah attempted to bring some reform, but the corruption of society was too entrenched. The spiritual leaders were confused and scattered. The prophets were lying to the people rather than proclaiming God's truth.

But to one prophet, Jeremiah, God promised a coming day when a righteous King would reign wisely "and do what is just and right in the land" (Jeremiah 23:5), and bring salvation to the people. "This is the name," Jeremiah was told, "by which he will be called: The LORD Our Righteousness" (verse 6).

The word *tsidkenu*, the Hebrew term in this verse for righteousness, means upright, straight, narrow. It means that a person's yes means yes and his no means no. It means not dealing in deception and not wavering in commitment to God's commandments. Having that righteousness means that we speak the truth even if people hate us for it.

When it comes to the righteousness of God and the commandments of His Word, there are no allowances for disobedience, no justifications for sin. God demands that His people uphold the morality of the Scriptures always and that they live in righteousness before Him. Only through God's provision of Christ can we do this.

In 1 Corinthians 1:30, the apostle Paul states that Christ has become our righteousness. By the gift of His indwelling Holy Spirit, Jesus enables us to walk daily in righteousness. The Holy Spirit convicts us of sin so that we know what is right and wrong, giving us the power to say no to temptation and yes to God's will for our lives.

The righteousness of God is the root of all integrity. It is the definition of all that is genuinely good in this life.

Praise Jehovah-Tsidkenu! Praise God our Righteousness!

———◆———

Your prophet Isaiah asks, "Who is this, robed in splendor, striding forward in the greatness of his strength?" And You answered him, "It is I, speaking in righteousness, mighty to save." Isaiah 63:1

For this I praise You, righteous Father, as I thank You for the gift of Your righteousness to me through Your Son, Jesus. I look forward to what this will mean in eternity: "In right-eousness I will see your face; when I awake, I will be satisfied with seeing your likeness." Psalm 17:15

Because of this, even now I "will celebrate your abun-dant goodness and joyfully sing of your righteousness." "Your right hand is filled with righteousness." Psalms 145:7; 48:10

JEHOVAH-SHAMMAH, GOD IS ALWAYS PRESENT

God is there for His children in every moment of every day. He never turns away, never puts us on hold. One of the last statements Jesus made to His disciples was this: "Surely I am with you always, to the very end of the age" (Matthew 28:20).

What an awesome truth that, in every moment and every circumstance, all the attributes of God embodied in His many names are available to us because He is Jehovah-Shammah, always present. This wonderful, awesome God—the Most High God who is our Healer, Victor, and Provider who gives us His peace, His holiness, and His righteousness—is with us always. All of God is with us all the time.

And His presence is eternal. In the praise songs of heaven, the Lord is described as the One "who was, and is, and is to come" (Revelation 4:8). He is also described as the One "who lives for ever and ever" (Revelation 4:9).

Praise Jehovah-Shammah! He is the One we can count on immediately and forever.

I can't help but believe that anytime we really begin to praise our Father and His Son and the Holy Spirit with the many names of God, we'll grow in our awareness of His presence with us. The more we catch a glimpse of all that God does and who He is, the more we'll want to praise Him. The more we know God through praising Him by name, the more we'll see Him at work in our lives, and the more we'll experience manifestations of His presence and power.

As you begin to praise aloud the names of God, I believe a spirit of revival will flood your soul. You'll find yourself energized and renewed. You'll find your attitude growing more hopeful and your faith growing more powerful.

Praise God, the God who reveals Himself to us through His names! When we praise God, let's call Him by name.

———◆———

Lord, because You are Jehovah-Shammah, I know for certain: "I am always with you; you hold me by my right hand. You guide me with your counsel, and afterward you will take me into glory." Psalm 73:23-24

"*If I go up to the heavens, you are there; if I make my bed in the depths, you are there. If I rise on the wings of the dawn, if I settle on the far side of the sea, even there your hand will guide me, your right hand will hold me fast.*"
Psalm 139:8-10

I speak Your praise, Elohim, El-Shaddai, Lord Jehovah:
"*Great is our Lord and mighty in power; his understanding has no limit.*" Psalm 147:5

PART III

THE BLESSINGS OF PRAISE

Praise the LORD, O my soul,
and forget not all his benefits.

PSALM 103:2

PRAISE DEFEATS THE ENEMY

Praise activates God's power in our lives, and nowhere is this more evident than in the realm of spiritual warfare. Praising God empowers us to defeat the devil.

Praise speaks the truth about God, something the devil cannot stand to hear. Satan's specialty is lies, and he cannot abide the truth about God's nature, God's deeds, and God's loving relationship with His people.

Satan is "the foe and the avenger," to use David's words from Psalm 8:2, and in praising God we proclaim His victory over this enemy. It's no accident that this psalm begins with David's proclamation of praise: "O LORD, our Lord, how majestic is your name in all the earth!" (8:1). Then David goes on to say,

From the lips of children and infants
>	you have ordained praise
because of your enemies,
>	to silence the foe and the avenger. (Psalm 8:2)

David may well have written this after defeating Goliath, the giant who sought to avenge the Philistines' previous defeats at the hands of Israel. Satan seeks a similar vengeance today. He lost the spiritual war at Calvary and has been seeking vengeance on believers ever since. He tries to enslave our bodies with addictions and excesses, our minds with heresies and paralyzing doubts, our spirits with guilt and shame. Satan seeks to take away our joy, rip apart our families, and wreck our relationship with Christ Jesus and His church.

The story of David and Goliath foreshadows the ultimate spiritual battle waged a thousand years later between Christ and Satan. In fact, David's defeat of Goliath is a model for our spiritual warfare today. Just as Goliath mocked and taunted the Israelites (see 1 Samuel 17), so Satan mocks and taunts us today. Will we stand up in indignation and righteousness, as David did? Or will we cower in fear, just as King Saul and the rest of the Israelite army did?

It's time to call upon the powers of heaven and humble ourselves before God, crying out, "O LORD, our Lord, how majestic is your name in all the earth!" (Psalm 8:1). It's time we see God as the victor over all the enemies who seek to take vengeance on the Lord's people.

Yes, Lord, "From the lips of children and infants you have ordained praise because of your enemies, to silence the foe and the avenger." Psalm 8:2

"How awesome are your deeds! So great is your power that your enemies cringe before you." "Who knows the power of your anger? For your wrath is as great as the fear that is due you." Psalms 66:3; 90:11

"Your hand will lay hold on all your enemies; your right hand will seize your foes." Psalm 21:8

IN THE BATTLE, CHILDLIKE FAITH

When the Pharisees rebuked Jesus during His triumphant entry into Jerusalem, He quoted to them David's praise for God in Psalm 8—"From the lips of children and infants you have ordained praise" (Matthew 21:16). What did Jesus mean? And what did David mean when he first sang those words?

Think for a moment about the faith of a young child. A child doesn't have doubts about whether God can do certain things. A child simply loves and believes and hopes. And so must we. The great strength of our praise in spiritual warfare is that by it we declare with childlike faith that God loves us and has gained the victory over Satan. God loves and God wins. Period.

When you're faced with a spiritual struggle—discouragement or temptation, fear or doubt—the best course of action is to exalt the position of God as the great victor in the battle against Satan. Praise God for sending Jesus to win the eternal war over your soul. Praising God will make the difference between winning or losing in every spiritual conflict you encounter.

Satan ultimately lost in his showdown with Jesus at the cross, and he continues to lose as believers take authority over the territory he controls on this earth—including his control of human hearts and minds.

God secured our salvation through Christ, and that is our power against Satan's attacks. Praise God, therefore, for raising Jesus from the dead so that you have the hope of eternal life. Praise Him because you heard the gospel, and because He convicted you of your sinful nature by the power of His Holy Spirit. Then praise God for securing once and for all the redemption of all who believe in Jesus. Praise Him because He loves you enough to lead you daily so you might be conformed to the image of Christ.

In the midst of spiritual warfare, praise God because Satan is our *defeated* foe forever. Praise God because we'll live in the light of His glory for all eternity.

◆

"Praise be to the LORD, for he showed his wonderful love to me." "He put a new song in my mouth, a hymn of praise to our God." Psalms 31:21; 40:3

"You give us victory over our enemies, you put our adversaries to shame." Psalm 44:7

"Even though I walk through the valley of the shadow of death, I will fear no evil, for you are with me." Psalm 23:4

"I will extol the LORD at all times; his praise will always be on my lips." Psalm 34:1

KNOWING HIS LOVE

The more we praise God for who He is, the more awesome He becomes in our understanding. Then the question comes to us: Why should this holy, perfect, all-wise God care about each of us? Why should He care about *any* human being?

There's no explanation for why God desires to be in relationship with you other than this one truth: He loves you unconditionally. There isn't anything you have done to warrant His love. It truly is a free and undeserved gift from God.

So many people engage in countless good works in order to try to earn enough points to win God's love. All the while, they don't realize that they *already* have His love and His attention.

They have the promise of His salvation held out to them with the open arms of Jesus on the cross.

What motivated Jesus to come to earth to die an agonizing death so that you might be spared the eternal consequences of your sin? What motivated Him to then send the Holy Spirit to seal your belief in Him? There is only one answer: love.

Everything Jesus did on earth was a reflection of God's love, giving us a picture of that love in terms that we can understand. Jesus hugged little children, dealt tenderly with those who confessed their sins, healed the sick, gave hope to the downtrodden, delivered those who were oppressed and possessed by demons, and set free those who were trapped by shame and guilt. In Jesus, we see love. And Jesus said, "Anyone who has seen me has seen the Father" (John 14:9).

"God is love," the apostle John wrote in 1 John 4:8, then he told how he knew that was true:

> This is how God showed his love among us: He sent
> his one and only Son into the world that we might live
> through him. This is love: not that we loved God, but
> that he loved us and sent his Son as an atoning sacrifice
> for our sins. (verses 9-10)

There's no explanation for God's unconditional love or for the mercy, forgiveness, and grace that flow from it without limit. Praise God today for His infinite, unconditional, everlasting love!

—◆—

"Your love, O LORD, reaches to the heavens, your faithfulness to the skies." "Great is your love toward me; you have delivered me from the depths of the grave." Psalms 36:5; 86:13

"Because your love is better than life, my lips will glorify you." "I will declare that your love stands firm forever, that you established your faithfulness in heaven itself." "Your love, O LORD, endures forever." Psalms 63:3; 89:2; 138:8

EMPOWERED TO PRAY

The more we praise God, the more we realize that, not only does He know about our needs, but He also desires to provide all that we need. God wants us to ask Him to meet our needs, not so that He'll become better informed about them, but so that *we* will become more aware of what is truly burdening us and tugging at our hearts.

Praise puts us in a position to receive answers from God, praise expressed in words like these:

You are all-powerful, Father. You can do all things.

You are all-merciful to Your children, Father. You desire to bless us in all ways.

You are patient and forgiving, Father. You long to draw all Your children close to You.

By giving God such praise, we realize that He is already supremely concerned about and fully capable of handling any petition we could ever make.

But how can we know if our requests are within His will? We begin by finding in God's Word the promises that God makes to *all* believers, so that we can focus our prayers on them. Then we can make our petitions in light of the things that count for eternity. Remember that Jesus told His disciples to seek first God's kingdom and His righteousness (Matthew 6:33).

Paul told the Ephesians that he was asking God to give them "the Spirit of wisdom and revelation, so that you may know him better" (Ephesians 1:17). His constant prayer for the Thessalonians was "that our God may count you worthy of his calling, and that by his power he may fulfill every good purpose of yours and every act prompted by your faith" (2 Thessalonians 1:11).

Certainly the Lord desires to meet our practical needs, and we aren't condemned by God when we mention them. But when we redirect our petitions to those things that involve spiritual wholeness and deliverance from evil, we grow in faith and develop spiritual maturity.

"Great is the Lord and most worthy of praise; his greatness no one can fathom.... I will proclaim your great deeds."
Psalm 145:3,6

"O LORD…are you not the God who is in heaven?
You rule over all the kingdoms of the nations. Power and
might are in your hand, and no one can withstand you."
2 Chronicles 20:6

I acknowledge Your great plan and purpose for this
world, to bring You glory: "For as the soil makes the sprout
come up and a garden causes seeds to grow, so the Sovereign
LORD will make righteousness and praise spring up before
all nations." "For the earth will be filled with the know-
ledge of the glory of the LORD, as the waters cover the sea."
Isaiah 61:11; Habakkuk 2:14

ENERGIZED FAITH

Praise empowers our prayers and also builds up our faith so that when we make our petitions before God, we pray with expectancy and confidence that we will receive God's best.

Consider the person who praises God, saying: "You are mighty, O Lord. You have made heaven and earth. You're the Author and Finisher of all faith, the Creator and Sustainer of all that is good. You are almighty God." How can a person who praises the Lord in that way then pray, "God, I hope You'll meet my need"?

Our praise builds up our faith, putting us in a position to pray, "*All* things are possible for my God." That was the mind-set of the apostle Paul when he wrote from a prison cell, "I can do everything through him who gives me strength" (Philippians 4:13).

Time and again we find in the Scriptures the admonition to pray with faith:

> If you believe, you will receive whatever you ask
> for in prayer. (Matthew 21:22)

> If any of you lacks wisdom, he should ask God,
> who gives generously to all without finding fault,
> and it will be given to him. But when he asks, he
> must believe and not doubt, because he who doubts
> is like a wave of the sea, blown and tossed by the
> wind. (James 1:5-6)

It is those who pray with faith who see God break the strongholds of the enemy. It takes faith to declare that you are God's property and the devil is a trespasser. It takes faith to confess that your body is the temple of the Holy Spirit who lives in you and works through you. It takes faith to stand against the enemy of your mind and body.

The assault against us is spiritual; our weapons of praise and prayer are also spiritual. When our faith is founded on the goodness and power of our mighty and unconquerable Savior and Lord, our faith is likewise mighty and unconquerable.

———◆———

I praise and thank You, God, for all that You do to nurture my faith.

I praise You, Father in heaven, for giving me the ability to respond to You in faith, for Your Son, Jesus, said, "No one can come to me unless the Father who sent me draws him." John 6:44

I praise You, Jesus, as the Author and Perfecter of my faith. Hebrews 12:2

And I praise You, Holy Spirit, for testifying within my spirit that I am a child of God. Romans 8:16

BOLDNESS IN ACTION

Praise puts us in the position of truly believing that the One within us "is greater than the one who is in the world" (1 John 4:4). Praise gives us "confidence to enter the Most Holy Place by the blood of Jesus," allowing us to "draw near to God with a sincere heart in full assurance of faith" and to "hold unswervingly to the hope we profess, for he who promised is faithful." (Hebrews 10:19,22-23).

When Peter and John were arrested for healing a lame man outside the temple in Jerusalem, the authorities warned them never to preach about Jesus again. John and Peter went back and reported this to the other believers. Rather than cower in fear, they raised their voices in praise and bold prayer:

Sovereign Lord…you made the heaven and the earth and the sea, and everything in them. You spoke by the Holy Spirit through the mouth of your servant, our father David:

"Why do the nations rage
    and the peoples plot in vain?
The kings of the earth take their stand
    and the rulers gather together
against the Lord
    and against his Anointed One."

Indeed Herod and Pontius Pilate met together with the Gentiles and the people of Israel in this city to conspire against your holy servant Jesus, whom you anointed. They did what your power and will had decided beforehand should happen. Now, Lord, consider their threats and enable your servants to speak your word with great boldness. Stretch out your hand to heal and perform miraculous signs and wonders through the name of your holy servant Jesus. (Acts 4:24-30)

Afterward, "the place where they were meeting was shaken. And they were all filled with the Holy Spirit and spoke the word of God boldly" (4:31).

Are you under attack? Are you feeling defeated? Are you tempted to compromise or give up? There is only one thing to do:

Sing praises to the Lord! Your praises will lead you to pray bold prayers, and God will respond by empowering you with His Holy Spirit.

Praise leads to faith, which leads to boldness in prayer, which leads to an outpouring of God's Spirit, which leads to confidence and boldness in action.

———

"My soul will boast in the LORD." "For you have been my hope, O Sovereign LORD, my confidence since my youth." Psalms 34:2; 71:5

Thank You, Lord, for increasing my confidence through the prayers You have answered. "When I called, you answered me; you made me bold and stouthearted." Psalm 138:3

And now by faith I say to You, "I trust in your unfailing love; my heart rejoices in your salvation." Psalm 13:5

THE POWER TO SERVE

Abundant praise leads to effective, merciful witnessing to those who don't know God and to consistent, love-laden ministry to the needy. Why? Because when we faithfully exalt the goodness and forgiveness and protection of God, we realize that we're the recipients of these blessings in His tender care. We develop a growing desire to give tender care to others and to lead them to God so they also will receive His blessings.

When we focus on how wonderful it is to be called a child of God and we recognize the awesome reality that we've been saved from everlasting hell, we're driven to lead others to Christ so they, too, might be saved.

Throughout the Old Testament, to worship God was to

"serve" Him by doing those things that were pleasing to Him—to offer the sacrifices of praise that He desired, to make the sacrificial gifts that He commanded, to engage in righteous living, and to meet the needs of widows and orphans and others in need. Worship was an outward action, not simply words that were spoken.

So, too, is our worship today. When we walk away from a time of praise, we're to put our praise into action—using our hands and feet to show others that we truly believe what we've said about God.

We say to Jesus, "You are God incarnate. You're our Savior. You died to pay in full the debt for our sin. You're the only way to a relationship with God. You are the Lord." When we walk away from praising Jesus in that way, our next task is to live in such a way that we express those realities in our behavior and also to say those same things to someone who doesn't know Jesus as Savior or who is discouraged in his faith walk.

What we believe about Jesus becomes what we praise Jesus for, and then our praise becomes the pattern for the way we live and for our witness to others.

Our ultimate expression of praise to God is a life that is obedient to His written commandments and to the daily guidance of the Holy Spirit. This is a life of praise.

———◆———

"No one is like you, O LORD; you are great, and your name is mighty in power." "Ah, Sovereign LORD, you have made the

heavens and the earth by your great power and outstretched arm. Nothing is too hard for you." Jeremiah 10:6; 32:17

"I will sing of the LORD's great love forever; with my mouth I will make your faithfulness known through all generations." Psalm 89:1

"I will declare your name to my brothers; in the congregation I will praise you." Psalm 22:22